Schott New York

Douglas J. Cuomo
b.1958

THE BOY'S NATURE
from *Doubt*

for mezzo-soprano and piano

Libretto by John Patrick Shanley

ED 30121

www.schott-music.com

Mainz · London · Madrid · New York · Paris · Prague · Tokyo · Toronto

for Denyce Graves

The Boy's Nature
from DOUBT

John Patrick Shanley

Douglas J. Cuomo

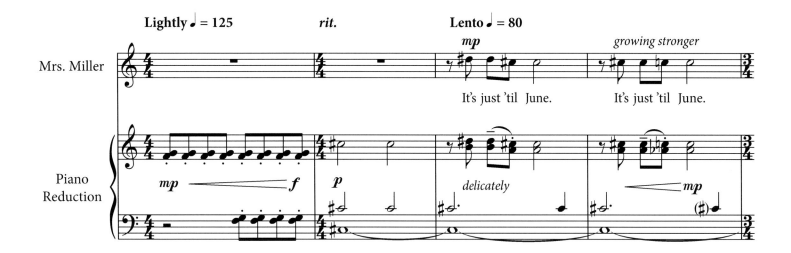

ED 30121

You can't hold a child re-spon-si-ble for what God gave him to be. But then there's the boy's na-ture. The boy's na-ture.

(ossia)
For - get it, then.

For - get it, then.

For - get it, then.

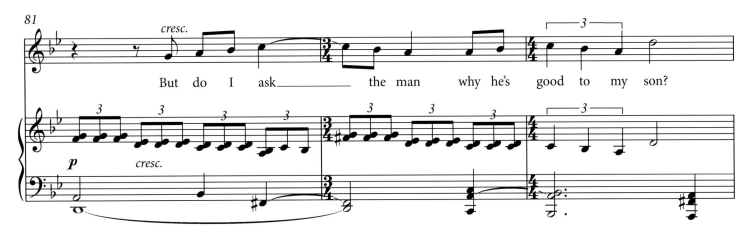

But do I ask_____ the man why he's good to my son?

No. No. No. I___ don't care why.___

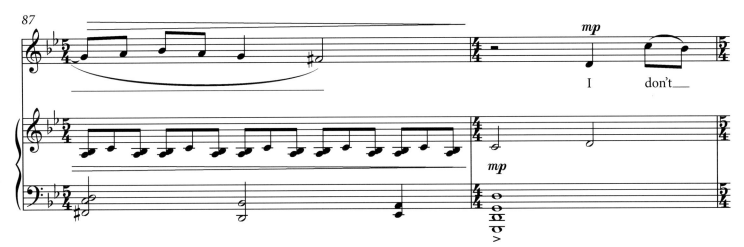

I don't___

care why.___

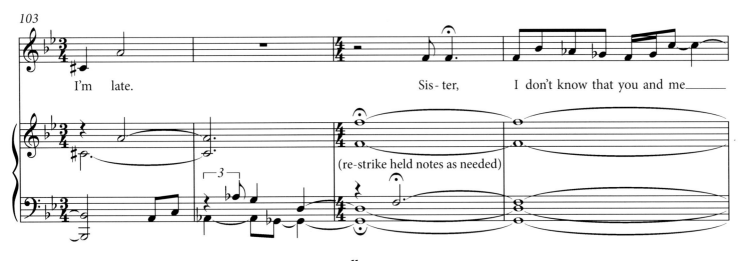

I'm late. Sis - ter, I don't know that you and me____

(re-strike held notes as needed)

colla voce

____ are on the same side.____ I'll be stand-ing here____with my son____ and those who are good____

____ with my son. It would be nice to see you____ there.____

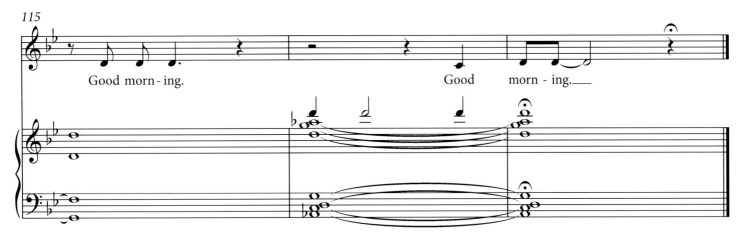

Good morn - ing. Good morn - ing.____